Colophon

©Mathias Jansson (2025)

"From Illusion to Immersion: AR and VR in Contemporary Art"

ISBN: 978-91-86915-83-4

Published by:

 "jag behöver inget förlag"

c/o Mathias Jansson

Tvärvägen 23

232 52 Åkarp

SWEDEN

http://mathiasjansson72.blogspot.se/

Print: Lulu.com

Disclaimer: This book is written with help of ChatGPT. The author has previously conducted extensive research on the subject and has also contributed texts about AR and VR Art in anthologies and journals. The essays have been improved, edited and proofread by the author before publishing.

Contents

Introduction: The Ancient Dream of Illusion 3

Chapter 1: From Shadows to Simulations: A History of Immersive Art 5

Chapter 2: The Birth of Virtual Reality: From the Sword of Damocles to Oculus 10

Chapter 3: Artists Enter the Virtual World................... 14

Chapter 4: Acute Art: Bringing VR Art to the Public...... 20

Chapter 5: A New Generation of VR Artists................. 25

Chapter 6: Painting in Virtual Space: Google Tilt Brush 31

Chapter 7: From Overlay to Immersion – The Story of Augmented Reality 33

Chapter 8: Immersion in Isolation – How COVID-19 Transformed VR and AR Art 37

Chapter 9: How AR Art Entered the Art Scene............. 40

Chapter 10: Augmented Reality as a Tool for Activism 44

Chapter 11: Augmented Realities – KAWS, Nina Chanel Abney, and Lauren Moffatt 47

Chapter 12: Museums, Art History, and Augmented Reality.. 50

Chapter 13: Beyond VR and AR – Defining Immersive Art Through Experience 53

Introduction: The Ancient Dream of Illusion

The story of immersive art does not begin with digital headsets, holograms, or projection mapping. It begins in antiquity, where artists, philosophers, and architects first grappled with the question of how images might create other realities. Long before "virtual reality" became a technical term, humanity imagined and constructed environments that blurred the boundaries between the real and the illusory.

Zeuxis and Parrhasius: The Contest of Illusion

In ancient Greece, two painters — Zeuxis and Parrhasius — became legendary for their skill in naturalistic representation. Their friendly rivalry culminated in a contest that has been retold for centuries. Zeuxis painted grapes so lifelike that birds swooped down to eat them. Confident of victory, he turned to examine Parrhasius' work, only to try to draw back a curtain — which itself was part of the painting. Deceived not just by representation but by the illusion of space, Zeuxis conceded defeat.

This anecdote reveals more than a witty exchange between artists; it marks the beginning of an artistic obsession with creating images that do not merely depict reality but *replace* it. The story of the curtain resonates with our contemporary encounters with VR headsets and AR overlays: a reminder that art has always sought to trick the senses and transport us beyond the visible world.

Each age has invented its own methods of creating virtual spaces, engaging the senses, and shaping collective imagination. This book traces the long arc of immersive art, from early visions of illusion to today's AR and VR practices. It explores how artists, museums, and festivals experiment with these technologies, why audiences are drawn to them, and what makes this form of art unique. Ultimately, it argues that AR and VR are not isolated innovations, but the continuation of an artistic dream as old as culture itself: the dream of entering another world.

Chapter 1: From Shadows to Simulations: A History of Immersive Art

The dream of stepping into another world is not unique to our digital age. Across history, artists, architects, philosophers, and inventors have devised ways to create spaces that dissolve the boundary between illusion and reality. From Plato's cave to the early days of cinema, each epoch has experimented with forms of immersion that anticipated the virtual realities we experience today.

Plato's Cave: Shadows as Early Immersion

The story begins with Plato's allegory of the cave, written in the 4th century BCE. In his famous thought experiment, prisoners are chained in a cavern, able to see only the shadows cast on the wall before them. For the captives, these flickering silhouettes constitute reality itself. Only when one prisoner escapes does he discover the "real" world beyond the cave.

This allegory has often been read as a metaphor for enlightenment, but it can also be understood as an early meditation on immersive environments. The cave presents spectators with a constructed reality — an environment where perception is manipulated and belief is suspended. Like today's virtual headsets, it demonstrates the profound power of images to shape human experience.

Trompe-l'œil and the Renaissance Perspective

The Renaissance brought new technical tools to the dream of immersion. The invention of linear perspective in the 15th century allowed artists like Brunelleschi, Masaccio, and later Leonardo da Vinci to create images that opened flat surfaces into convincing three-dimensional spaces. A painting could now function like a window into another world.

Trompe-l'œil — literally "to deceive the eye" — became a celebrated technique, with artists designing ceilings that seemed to dissolve into the heavens or walls that opened into imaginary architecture. Churches, palaces, and theaters transformed into hybrid spaces where real and painted architecture blended seamlessly. The Renaissance thus marked the "birth of virtual space," where illusionistic representation became a dominant artistic ambition.

Baroque Theatrical Machines and Scenery

By the 17th century, art and technology converged in theatrical spectacles. Baroque theaters used elaborate stage machinery, shifting scenery, and mechanical devices to transport audiences into mythological landscapes or celestial realms. Trapdoors, moving clouds, and rotating stage sets created experiences of wonder and disorientation.

These innovations were not merely decorative but immersive strategies designed to dissolve the distinction between stage and audience. The theater became a prototype for later immersive technologies, a carefully orchestrated environment where illusion was experienced collectively and viscerally.

The Panorama and Diorama: 18th–19th Century Worlds

In the late 18th century, a new medium took Europe by storm: the panorama. Visitors stepped into circular buildings where vast 360-degree paintings surrounded them, creating the sensation of being inside a city, a battlefield, or a landscape. The panorama democratized immersion, offering audiences the thrill of travel, spectacle, and history without leaving their hometowns.

Related forms, such as the diorama, combined painted scenes with lighting effects and sound to simulate changes in weather, time of day, or atmosphere. These environments anticipated modern virtual worlds, using light and illusion to generate a sense of presence and emotional engagement.

Early Cinema: The Dream of Total Immersion

With the invention of cinema at the end of the 19th century, the dream of total immersion entered the modern age. The moving image amplified the power of illusion, adding motion, narrative, and later sound to the immersive experience. Early screenings of the Lumière brothers' *Arrival of a Train at La Ciotat* (1896) famously startled audiences, who felt the locomotive rushing toward them.

Throughout the 20th century, cinema continued to push toward immersion: widescreen formats, surround sound, and experiments like Cinerama and 3D aimed to engulf spectators in the world of the film. Although cinema remained framed by the screen, its ambition was always to transport audiences beyond it.

The Sensorama: A Prototype of Virtual Reality

In 1962, filmmaker and inventor Morton Heilig unveiled the Sensorama, often described as the first attempt at a true virtual reality system. The device was a large arcade-style machine that immersed a single user in a multi-sensory experience. Sitting in the chair, the participant watched 3D stereoscopic films while feeling vibrations in the seat, smelling scents released from hidden cartridges, and hearing surround sound audio.

One of the films simulated a motorcycle ride through New York City, complete with wind on the face, engine vibrations, and city smells. Heilig described the Sensorama as an "experience theater" — an early effort to engage all the senses in a synthetic world. Though the machine was never commercially successful, it embodied the same aspirations that continue to drive VR and AR today: to create environments so convincing they blur the line between physical and virtual experience.

Continuity of a Dream

From the flickering shadows of Plato's cave to Heilig's Sensorama, the history of immersive art reveals a continuous trajectory. Each era developed its own strategies and technologies to simulate other worlds: perspective in Renaissance painting, theatrical machines in the Baroque, panoramic illusions in the 19th century, cinematic spectacle in the 20th.

While the tools have changed, the underlying impulse has remained constant: the human desire to transcend the here and now, to step into imagined spaces, and to lose oneself — at least for a moment — in another reality.

Chapter 2: The Birth of Virtual Reality: From the Sword of Damocles to Oculus

Virtual reality, as we understand it today, emerged not from the imagination of painters or theater directors, but from the laboratories of engineers and computer scientists in the mid-20th century. The dream of entering artificial worlds began to take technical form in the 1960s, when computers became powerful enough to generate interactive graphics. What had long been a metaphor or illusion was about to become a tangible experience.

The Sword of Damocles: The First Head-Mounted Display

In 1968, Ivan Sutherland, often called the father of computer graphics, created what is considered the first true virtual reality system. His invention was a bulky head-mounted display (HMD) connected to a computer, nicknamed the *Sword of Damocles* because of the heavy apparatus suspended from the ceiling above the user's head.

Through the headset, participants could see simple wireframe graphics that shifted perspective as they moved their heads. By today's standards, the imagery was primitive, but it marked a radical breakthrough: for the first time, a person could look around inside a computer-generated 3D environment. This was not merely an image but an interactive space — a prototype of the virtual realities to come.

Pioneers of Virtual Reality: Jaron Lanier and VPL Research

In the 1980s, the term *virtual reality* entered public consciousness, largely thanks to the work of Jaron Lanier. A musician, programmer, and visionary, Lanier founded VPL Research in 1984, one of the first companies to develop and commercialize VR equipment.

VPL created devices such as the DataGlove, which allowed users to interact with digital objects through hand gestures, and the EyePhone, an early VR headset. Lanier's experiments fused technology with imagination: VR, he argued, was not just a tool for simulation but a new artistic and cultural medium. In interviews and writings, he described virtual reality as a space for creativity, shared worlds, and human expression, helping to frame VR as more than just a technological novelty.

The First Commercial Models

By the late 1980s and early 1990s, VR began to reach the public. In 1991, a British company called Virtuality introduced VR arcade machines that brought immersive experiences to the public. For a few pounds, players could use a headset and step into polygonal 3D battle arenas, racing simulations, or cooperative adventures. The experience was rudimentary — blocky graphics, heavy equipment, limited responsiveness — but it was unforgettable for many who encountered VR for the first time.

Around the same time, consumer electronics companies sensed a new market. Sega announced the *Sega VR* headset for its Genesis console in 1993, promising a cheap home version of the arcade experience. Nintendo followed with the *Virtual Boy* in 1995, a red-and-black tabletop headset that offered stereoscopic 3D gaming. Both were commercial failures: the technology was uncomfortable, the visuals underwhelming, and the public quickly lost interest.

The 1990s VR boom collapsed almost as quickly as it began, leaving behind a cultural residue of "cyberspace" imagery in films like *The Lawnmower Man* (1992), *Johnny Mnemonic* (1995), and *The Matrix* (1999). VR became a symbol of technological futurism — but for the average person, it remained out of reach.

The Rebirth: Oculus and the 2010s VR Renaissance

The idea of VR never disappeared, however. In research labs and specialized industries such as aviation and military training, VR continued to evolve. The turning point came in 2012, when Palmer Luckey launched the *Oculus Rift* through a Kickstarter campaign. Leveraging advances in mobile phone screens and motion sensors, Oculus delivered smoother, cheaper, and more immersive experiences than previous headsets.

Facebook's acquisition of Oculus in 2014 signaled that VR was once again seen as a technology with mass potential. Other companies quickly followed: HTC released the *Vive*, Sony introduced *PlayStation VR*, and Google and Samsung experimented with mobile-based headsets.

This time, VR entered living rooms, classrooms, and galleries. While sales have fluctuated, the ecosystem of VR hardware and software has grown dramatically, supported by gaming companies, tech giants, and a growing community of independent developers.

From Hype to Everyday Use

By the 2020s, VR had found its place not as a universal replacement for the screen, but as a specialized medium: powerful in gaming, training, design, and — increasingly — the arts. The commercial infrastructure gave artists and museums access to tools that were once limited to research labs, paving the way for a new generation of immersive artworks and exhibitions.

Chapter 3: Artists Enter the Virtual World

As VR entered the consumer market, artists and cultural institutions quickly recognized its potential. For some, VR was a new medium of artistic expression; for others, it was a tool for education, storytelling, and preservation. What united these experiments was the conviction that VR could offer experiences that were impossible through traditional media.

CAVE (Cave Automatic Virtual Environment)

One of the most influential systems was the CAVE (Cave Automatic Virtual Environment), developed at the University of Illinois in 1992. Unlike head-mounted displays, the CAVE was a room-sized cube where images were projected onto walls, floor, and ceiling, surrounding participants in a 3D environment. Users wore lightweight 3D glasses and could walk inside the projected world, creating a shared immersive experience.

Artists and scientists collaborated on projects in the CAVE, from abstract explorations of data to immersive narratives. The system became a model for how VR could move beyond solitary headsets to collective experiences, where immersion was as much about space and community as about technology.

Other artists in the 1990s used VR to question perception, identity, and embodiment. Char Davies' *Osmose* (1995), for example, employed a head-mounted display and a breath-and-balance interface, allowing participants to float through luminous virtual environments. Rather than simulating physical reality, *Osmose* sought to evoke altered states of consciousness, positioning VR as a poetic and experiential medium rather than a purely technical one.

Dominique Gonzalez-Foerster – *Endodrome* at the Venice Biennale

By the late 2010s, VR had become a staple of major art festivals and biennales. The Venice Biennale introduced an XR section, Sundance Film Festival launched its *New Frontier* program, and the Tribeca Film Festival created a dedicated immersive category.

Virtual reality has gradually entered the highest levels of the art world, and the Venice Biennale has played a key role in legitimizing it as an artistic medium. In 58th Venice Biennale, 2019, the French artist Dominique Gonzalez-Foerster presented her first VR work, titled *Endodrome*. This marked a milestone: VR was no longer just a technological experiment or a niche gallery attraction — it had become a recognized form of contemporary art showcased on one of the world's most prestigious stages.

Endodrome is a multi-user VR experience that allows five participants simultaneously to enter a virtual environment. Once inside, visitors are guided through a trance-like journey, designed to evoke a meditative and introspective state. Gonzalez-Foerster frames this work as an exploration of space, perception, and consciousness, inviting participants to inhabit alternative mental states inspired by her own experiences with cognitive "trance."

The virtual environment is carefully choreographed to heighten immersion. Visuals unfold in subtle, fluid sequences, guiding the user inward rather than overwhelming the senses with spectacle. A specially composed soundscape, created by a collaborating musician and writer, complements the visual experience, shaping the temporal and emotional flow of the journey. Sound and imagery work together to produce a holistic encounter that blurs the line between inner and outer worlds, physical and virtual presence.

Endodrome exemplifies how VR in contemporary art is not just about creating alternative realities for their own sake. It demonstrates a deeply conceptual approach: using immersive technology to probe consciousness, meditative states, and the subjective perception of space. By presenting such a work at the Venice Biennale, Gonzalez-Foerster signals that VR can operate on the same level as painting, sculpture, or installation art — offering aesthetic, experiential, and intellectual engagement simultaneously.

Laurie Anderson and Hsin-Chien Huang: Poetic Journeys in VR

The renowned performance artist Laurie Anderson and multimedia artist Hsin-Chien Huang have collaborated for several years, exploring the intersections of technology, storytelling, and immersive art. In recent years, their shared focus has shifted toward virtual reality, creating works that invite viewers into poetic, meditative journeys through imagined spaces.

One of their most celebrated collaborations is *Chalkroom* (2017), a VR experience that emphasizes introspection and exploration of inner spaces. In this work, visitors wander through a vast, text-based environment: black walls filled with floating white letters, words, and narratives. The imagery evokes the appearance of old-school chalkboards, linking the virtual environment to memory, learning, and reflection. Participants are free to navigate the space at their own pace, uncovering stories and connecting with the poetic landscape in a deeply personal way. In *Chalkroom*, the act of reading, moving, and observing becomes a meditative practice, turning the visitor into both explorer and part of the narrative itself.

Another remarkable work by the duo is *To the Moon* (2018), in which the participant assumes the role of an astronaut landing on the lunar surface. This VR piece is described as a spiritual meditation on the time we inhabit, offering a contemplative perspective on life on

Earth. The experience draws inspiration from the few humans who have stood on the Moon and looked back at our planet: many report that this view profoundly transformed their perception of Earth and our place in the universe. *To the Moon* asks whether virtual reality can replicate a similar effect — offering participants an expanded sense of scale, reflection, and presence.

Antony Gormley's *Lunatick* and the VR Journey Beyond Earth

In a similar vein, the British sculptor Antony Gormley and astrophysicist Dr. Priyamvada Natarajan, in collaboration with the company AcuteArt, created *Lunatick* (2019). The work begins on an abandoned island in the Pacific Ocean, from which the participant is launched into space. After orbiting the Earth, the journey culminates with a landing on the Moon, where viewers can explore the lunar landscape from a perspective that is both intimate and awe-inspiring.

Lunatick draws a conceptual line back to early cinematic explorations of space, most notably Georges Méliès' *A Trip to the Moon* (1902). Méliès' film, groundbreaking for its time, tells the story of a group of scientists whose rocket is fired from a giant cannon to the Moon, where they encounter fantastical creatures and landscapes. The film's inventive use of special effects paved the way for imaginative storytelling in cinema. Today, VR allows contemporary artists like Laurie Anderson and Antony Gormley to reimagine the same journey, not merely as a narrative to watch but as an immersive experience to inhabit.

Where Méliès' Moon was a painted set and camera trickery, *Lunatick* and *To the Moon* transport participants into fully navigable virtual worlds. Both works explore scale, perspective, and the emotional impact of viewing Earth from space, inviting reflections on humanity, environment, and the cosmos. In this way, VR becomes a modern continuation of a centuries-long artistic and scientific fascination with space travel, imagination, and the transcendence of everyday perception.

Chapter 4: Acute Art: Bringing VR Art to the Public

Acute Art was founded in 2017 by the art collectors Gerard De Geer and Jacob De Geer with the vision of bridging the gap between contemporary art and emerging digital technologies. In 2019 Daniel Birnbaum joined as curator and creative director.

The platform collaborates with leading international artists to create immersive VR and AR experiences, making cutting-edge art accessible to audiences beyond museum walls. Through their Acute Art app, available on smartphones and VR headsets, users worldwide can explore works by renowned artists such as Marina Abramović, Jeff Koons, Anish Kapoor, Antony Gormley, KAWS, and Olafur Eliasson. Acute Art's mission is to democratize access to immersive art, allowing anyone to experience, interact with, and reflect on art in ways that were previously only possible in physical gallery spaces. In addition to Antony Gormley and his VR work *Lunatick* (2019), Acute Art has collaborated with several other prominent artists, including:

Marina Abramović: *Rising* – Confronting Climate Change Through VR

In her first foray into virtual reality, the pioneering performance artist Marina Abramović created *Rising* (2018), a VR experience that transforms the viewer into an active participant in an urgent environmental narrative. The work immerses participants in a scenario of rising sea levels, where they find themselves standing in a flooded environment that threatens to overwhelm them.

Rising draws on Abramović's long-standing interest in the body, endurance, and presence, translating these themes into a digital context. In the VR space, participants are confronted with the immediate, visceral consequences of climate change: water gradually engulfs the surroundings, creating a sense of vulnerability, urgency, and responsibility. The experience combines visual and auditory elements — from the lapping of water to the subtle creaking of submerged structures — to heighten immersion and emotional engagement.

By placing the viewer directly inside the environmental crisis, Abramović transforms abstract statistics into a personal, embodied experience. The work encourages reflection on humanity's relationship with the natural world and the consequences of inaction, demonstrating how VR can amplify the emotional and cognitive impact of artistic interventions.

Rising has been presented through the Acute Art platform, which allows users worldwide to access the work via VR headsets or even mobile devices. This accessibility expands the reach of the artwork, enabling it to function not only as a gallery installation but also as a tool for awareness and activism.

Through *Rising*, Abramović shows that VR is not merely a medium for spectacle or simulation — it can also serve as a platform for ethical engagement and environmental consciousness, merging immersive technology with urgent contemporary themes.

Anish Kapoor: *Into Yourself, Fall* – Exploring Depth and Perception in VR

Renowned for his monumental sculptures and explorations of space, light, and materiality, Anish Kapoor extends his artistic practice into the realm of virtual reality with *Into Yourself, Fall* (2019). This immersive VR experience invites viewers to embark on a journey into a reflective, meditative space, where perception, depth, and form are continuously questioned and transformed.

In *Into Yourself, Fall*, participants navigate through a series of abstract, mirrored environments that respond to their movements and gaze. Surfaces seem to fold into themselves, voids appear to extend infinitely, and gravity feels mutable, creating a sensation of both vertigo and introspection. Kapoor's signature interest in the interplay of presence, absence, and the infinite is reimagined in virtual space, allowing users to physically inhabit forms and spaces that would be impossible in the physical world.

The work emphasizes embodiment and subjective perception, encouraging viewers to consider how their own position and movement influence the visual and spatial experience. By translating his sculptural vocabulary into VR, Kapoor transforms the medium into a site of reflection and perceptual experimentation, blurring the boundaries between digital and physical, object and environment, viewer and artwork.

Olafur Eliasson: *Your View Matter* (2022) – A Journey Through Geometry and Perception

In 2022, Danish–Icelandic artist Olafur Eliasson unveiled *Your View Matter*, an immersive virtual reality (VR) artwork that invites viewers into a series of six geometric spaces. Five of these spaces are based on Platonic solids—the tetrahedron, octahedron, icosahedron, dodecahedron, and cube—while the sixth is a sphere. These shapes, revered since antiquity for their symmetry and philosophical significance, serve as the foundation for Eliasson's exploration of spatial perception and bodily awareness in the digital realm.

The experience is designed to be navigated through movement: as participants walk through the virtual spaces and shift their perspectives, they encounter dynamic moiré patterns—visual distortions that emerge when similar patterns overlap. These patterns, some colorful and others starkly black and white, evolve in response to the viewer's movements, emphasizing the interplay between the observer and the observed. This interaction underscores Eliasson's long-standing interest in how perception is shaped by both the environment and the individual's physical presence.

Accompanied by a minimalist, pulsating soundtrack composed by Eliasson himself, *Your View Matter* encourages participants to engage actively with the virtual environment. The work challenges traditional notions of passive viewing, positioning the observer as an integral component of the artwork's unfolding. By doing so, Eliasson invites reflection on the nature of perception and the role of the viewer in constructing meaning within both physical and virtual spaces

Chapter 5: A New Generation of VR Artists

When VR first entered the art world, many of the pioneers were already established names in contemporary art. Artists such as Marina Abramović, Anish Kapoor, or Antony Gormley approached VR as an experimental extension of their existing practices. Their projects often felt like singular encounters—moments where a renowned artist "visited" the new medium to test its potential. These works were significant for drawing attention to VR within the museum and biennial context, but they often remained exceptions within otherwise broad careers.

By contrast, a younger generation of artists has emerged for whom VR is not a temporary experiment but a core medium of expression.

Rachel Rossin: Navigating Between the Virtual and the Real

One of the rising stars in contemporary VR art is the American artist, Rachel Rossin (b. 1987). In 2016, she became the first artist to hold a Virtual Reality residency at the New Museum in New York, producing the VR work *Man Mask* (2016). This piece was later included, in the free app First Look: Artists' VR, featuring six commissioned works by leading artists: Peter Burr with Porpentine Charity Heartscape, Jeremy Couillard, Jayson Musson, Jon Rafman, Rachel Rossin, and Jacolby Satterwhite, which allows audiences to explore immersive artworks on their smartphones.

Rossin's artistic practice fluidly traverses the boundary between virtual and physical realities. She combines VR environments with traditional painting on canvas or plexiglass, often shaped and sculpted according to her own body. This hybrid approach reflects her ongoing interest in how physical bodies relate to space, both in the real world and within digital landscapes.

In *Man Mask*, Rossin draws inspiration from the video game *Call of Duty: Black Ops*, using the bodies of players and game environments to construct a virtual world of her own design. The work explores embodiment, presence, and the spatial relationships of bodies within constructed realities, a recurring theme in her VR practice. Visitors navigating *Man Mask* are invited to consider how the digital body can expand, deform, or interact with space in ways that differ from physical experience.

Rossin's work exemplifies how contemporary VR art can intersect gaming, painting, and immersive environments, creating experiences that are at once visceral and intellectual. By merging digital and physical practice, she investigates not only the potential of VR as a medium but also the evolving relationship between human bodies and virtual spaces. Her art reflects a growing trend among contemporary VR artists: using immersive technology not just to simulate environments but to question how we inhabit and perceive space itself.

Jakob Kudsk Steensen – Virtual Ecologies

Among the younger generation of artists working with VR, Jakob Kudsk Steensen (b. 1987, Denmark) has also emerged as one of the most important figures. His practice centers on the intersection between technology, ecology, and storytelling. Using game engines, photogrammetry, and VR, Steensen creates immersive ecosystems that highlight the fragility of the natural world and invite audiences into poetic, slow-moving encounters with landscapes often overlooked or endangered.

Re-Animated (2018)

Jakob Kudsk Steensen's *Re-Animated* stands as one of his most widely recognized VR installations, offering a poetic encounter with extinction and memory. The work takes as its starting point the Kauai'O'o, a bird native to Hawaii whose last known song was recorded in 1987 by ornithologist David Boynton, just before the species disappeared forever. That recording, a fragile audio trace of a lost world, forms the emotional core of Steensen's project.

Through VR, visitors enter a digitally reconstructed rainforest, painstakingly built using 3D photogrammetry, animation, and ecological data. The lush environment teems with plant life and atmospheric soundscapes, enveloping the viewer in a world both real and imagined. As participants wander through this virtual ecosystem, they hear the

Kauai'O'o solitary call—an echo of a voice that will never again be heard in nature.

The work is not only an elegy for a vanished species but also a reflection on the limits of technology. VR cannot bring back the bird itself, but it can evoke a sense of intimacy with what has been lost, making the audience feel the absence more acutely. *Re-Animated* questions whether digital resurrection offers solace or only heightens our awareness of irreversible disappearance. In this way, the work becomes a meditation on the Anthropocene, digital memory, and humanity's role as both creator and destroyer.

Primal Tourism (2016)

In *Primal Tourism*, Steensen turns his attention to the future rather than the past, constructing a speculative vision of the island Bora-Bora in French Polynesia. The island, already a popular tourist destination, is imagined here as a place transformed by climate change and ecological upheaval. Through VR, the audience explores surreal, hybrid landscapes—at once natural and artificial—where tropical vegetation collides with futuristic architecture and eroded environments.

The title itself, *Primal Tourism*, suggests a paradox. Tourism is typically associated with leisure and escape, yet here it is tied to survival and displacement, reflecting how climate refugees might one day travel not for pleasure but for necessity. The VR environment places the viewer inside this tension: a destination both alluring and unsettling, familiar and alien.

Steensen describes himself as a "digital gardener." His VR works are not about spectacle or fast-moving narratives but about slowness, attention, and care. Unlike many blockbuster VR experiences, his art encourages meditative exploration, where viewers are not passive consumers but active participants, choosing how to wander through the reconstructed worlds.

What makes Steensen's contribution to VR art so important is his ability to merge scientific research with poetic immersion. At a time when climate change and mass extinction are pressing global issues, his VR worlds function as both aesthetic experiences and ecological reflections. By using the technology of game design for contemplative rather than competitive purposes, Steensen has opened a new space for VR art—one that is not only immersive but also profoundly environmental.

Jordan Wolfson: *Little Room*

Jordan Wolfson (b. 1980) has built his career on unsettling encounters with technology and the body. His VR work *Little Room* (2025), presented at the Fondation Beyeler during Art Basel, pushes this to new extremes.

The experience begins with a ritual of surveillance: visitors undergo a full-body scan with 96 cameras, creating a detailed 3D model uploaded into the VR system. Inside the headset, participants find themselves in a stark tiled room with one other person. The shock comes quickly—you inhabit the body of your partner while they occupy yours. A mirror drifts into view, forcing you to watch yourself being controlled by someone else, your mouth repeating Wolfson's prerecorded lines: *"God murdered me... Look at your hands, I love you. Look at your hands, I hate you."*

The horror is subtle but piercing: no gore, only the psychic violation of losing your own body. Unlike other VR artists who build immersive worlds, Wolfson uses estrangement. The minimal chamber enhances the dissonance, recalling Lygia Clark's body-centered experiments but shifting them into colder, more invasive territory.

Little Room transforms VR from a tool of wonder or empathy into a mirror of alienation. It is not an escape but a trap, leaving participants staring at themselves with an unnatural intensity—an unsettling form of digital narcissism that refuses resolution.

Chapter 6: Painting in Virtual Space: Google Tilt Brush

One of the milestones in the democratization of VR art came not from a museum or a gallery but from a tech company: Google Tilt Brush. Released in 2016, the software gave artists and designers the ability to paint in three-dimensional space using a VR headset and handheld controllers. Instead of working on a flat canvas, users could step inside their own creations, painting with light, fire, smoke, or even abstract particle effects that floated and shimmered in the air.

Tilt Brush opened up a new way of thinking about painting and sculpture: art no longer needed to be confined to two-dimensional surfaces or fixed physical spaces. With a headset, the artist could quite literally "walk through the brushstrokes." This shift marked VR not just as a medium for creating immersive environments, but also as a creative studio in itself.

Google Tilt Brush Artist-in-Residence Program (2016–2017) invited a group of artists and designers from diverse backgrounds to experiment with the medium. Participants included illustrators, game designers, and installation artists who tested the limits of VR painting, often blending it with animation and 3D sound. This program helped push Tilt Brush beyond novelty, showing its potential as a serious artistic instrument.

At Art Basel 2017, Google invited a group of contemporary artists to explore the creative potential of its VR painting tool Tilt Brush. Among them was Cao Fei, one of the most influential Chinese artists of her generation, celebrated for her ability to merge popular culture, digital aesthetics, and critical reflections on social change.

For Cao Fei, Tilt Brush was not simply a new medium, but a continuation of her long-standing interest in virtual worlds. Her earlier project *RMB City* (2009–2011), created within Second Life, built a sprawling digital metropolis as a playground for art and imagination. At Art Basel, she extended this exploration into fully immersive VR, using Tilt Brush to create dynamic drawings in space that viewers could walk around and experience as living environments rather than static images.

Tilt Brush's impact lies not only in the artworks produced with it but in how it lowered the threshold for entering VR art-making. Suddenly, VR creation was no longer the exclusive domain of coders, developers, or large studios. Instead, painters, illustrators, and even amateurs could experiment with immersive mark-making, reshaping the very idea of what it means to paint in the 21st century.

Chapter 7: From Overlay to Immersion – The Story of Augmented Reality

Virtual Reality (VR) and Augmented Reality (AR) are often spoken of in the same breath, but their approaches to digital experience are fundamentally different. VR is a total environment. When we put on a VR headset, we leave the physical world behind and enter a fully simulated space. Everything we see, hear, and sometimes even touch is designed and controlled by software. This creates the sense of *presence*—the feeling of being "inside" another reality.

AR, by contrast, is not about replacing reality but augmenting it. Through smartphones, tablets, or AR glasses, digital content is layered onto our physical surroundings. Instead of being cut off from the world, we continue to see it, but with added information, animations, or interactive objects. If VR asks us to step into another universe, AR asks us to look at our own world differently, reshaped by digital overlays.

This difference also means that AR and VR provoke different cultural and artistic responses. VR has often been connected with escapism, world-building, and immersion, while AR tends to emphasize context, site-specificity, and the merging of technology with everyday life.

The Early Visions of AR

The term *Augmented Reality* was first used in the early 1990s by researcher Tom Caudell, who described a digital display system for assisting Boeing engineers during airplane assembly. Instead of relying on printed manuals, workers could see instructions projected onto the parts they were working on, reducing errors and speeding up the process.

This industrial focus set the tone for the first wave of AR: it was a tool for specialists rather than a medium for the public. In the 1990s and early 2000s, AR found its place in military training, medical visualization, and industrial design. Bulky headsets and limited computing power kept it confined to labs and research centers.

Artists were intrigued but had little access to the technology. Those who experimented with AR often did so through site-specific installations using projectors or early head-mounted displays. The dream of merging the virtual with the everyday cityscape was there, but the tools were not yet in the hands of ordinary people.

AR Enters the Everyday

The 2000s saw the rise of smartphones, which suddenly put cameras, sensors, and portable computing power into millions of pockets. Developers began experimenting with simple AR applications: pointing a phone at a magazine page might trigger an animation; scanning a landmark could reveal hidden information. Companies like Layar (founded in 2009) tried to build AR browsers for urban environments, overlaying data on top of city streets.

These early apps were often more exciting as concepts than as daily utilities. Still, they marked a turning point: AR was no longer limited to research labs. Everyday users could now get a taste of the technology, even if it was rough and unreliable.

Pokémon Go and the AR Breakthrough

The true mass adoption of AR arrived in 2016 with Niantic's *Pokémon Go*. Suddenly, AR was not an abstract concept but a global cultural phenomenon. Millions of players took to the streets, parks, and squares in search of digital Pokémon, visible through their phones as if they inhabited the real world.

What made *Pokémon Go* revolutionary was not only its clever use of AR but also its blending of physical and social experience. The game encouraged people to explore their neighborhoods, meet strangers, and treat familiar spaces in new ways. Parks became battlegrounds, monuments became PokéStops, and entire cities transformed into playful hybrid environments.

It also proved that AR could scale. While earlier AR experiments were limited to small audiences, *Pokémon Go* demonstrated that millions could simultaneously share an AR experience, each seeing a version of the same digital layer mapped onto their physical surroundings.

AR as a Cultural and Artistic Tool

After *Pokémon Go*, AR was no longer a niche technology. Social media platforms quickly integrated AR filters, allowing users to alter their faces, bodies, and surroundings with a swipe. This democratization of AR brought it into everyday culture, where it became as much about identity play and self-expression as about information.

For artists and museums, AR suddenly became a new way to reach audiences. Instead of requiring visitors to come to a gallery, artworks could appear on smartphones anywhere. AR allowed sculptures to float in public squares, paintings to come alive in private homes, and performances to extend beyond the stage. Unlike VR, which still required specialized hardware, AR piggybacked on the devices people already carried.

Museums began experimenting with AR guides, where visitors could point their phones at artworks to unlock hidden layers of interpretation. Public art commissions embraced AR to create site-specific interventions without physically altering the environment. Artists like Cao Fei, Kaws, and many others have since embraced AR to create works that straddle both real and virtual presence.

Chapter 8: Immersion in Isolation – How COVID-19 Transformed VR and AR Art

When the COVID-19 pandemic struck in early 2020, museums and galleries across the world were forced to shut their doors. For the first time in modern history, the art world was cut off from its primary mode of experience: physical presence. Yet out of this crisis came an unexpected acceleration of interest in virtual and augmented reality art. Technologies once seen as experimental supplements to exhibitions suddenly became lifelines, offering audiences a way to continue engaging with art despite the isolation of lockdowns.

Museums in the Virtual Sphere

Institutions that had previously been slow to adopt immersive technologies found themselves experimenting out of necessity. The Smithsonian in Washington, D.C. launched expanded virtual tours, allowing audiences to navigate its galleries from home. The Louvre in Paris, facing massive losses in visitor numbers, opened up VR experiences of its most famous collections online. Even smaller regional museums began collaborating with platforms to digitize exhibitions and make them available in immersive formats.

The Rise of VR Exhibitions

One of the most important platforms during this period was Acute Art, which had already built a strong presence in the VR/AR field. During lockdown, they pivoted toward creating experiences specifically designed for remote audiences. Their app allowed users worldwide to download and explore works by artists like Olafur Eliasson, KAWS, Marina Abramović, and Anish Kapoor directly on their smartphones or VR headsets.

The exhibition *Unreal City* (2020) became a milestone. Initially planned as a large-scale public AR show along the Thames in London, it was reimagined during lockdown as Unreal City at Home. Visitors could download the Acute Art app and bring the exhibition into their own living rooms, parks, or gardens. By scanning their environment with a smartphone, people could suddenly see Kapoor's infinite voids or Eliasson's shifting geometries unfold before them. This shift democratized access: what had been limited to a city-specific event became a global experience.

Expanding Accessibility

The pandemic highlighted a fundamental potential of immersive art: accessibility. Audiences who might never travel to London, New York, or Venice could suddenly encounter high-profile works in their own homes. While the VR headset market remained niche, the widespread use of smartphones made AR art more accessible than ever. Museums and curators began to recognize that VR and AR were not just temporary substitutes during crisis—they could expand audiences permanently, reaching people far beyond the physical walls of cultural institutions.

Lasting Impact

As restrictions lifted, many museums and artists retained their interest in immersive formats. The lessons of lockdown proved that VR and AR could no longer be sidelined as gimmicks; they had shown their ability to carry art into times of crisis, to transcend geography, and to sustain cultural life even in isolation.

The COVID-19 pandemic thus became a turning point for immersive art. What began as an emergency solution evolved into a broader vision: a world where art is no longer bound by location, where digital and physical exhibitions coexist, and where the immersive experience is available not only to the privileged visitor but to anyone, anywhere.

Chapter 9: How AR Art Entered the Art Scene

For a long time, Augmented Reality (AR) was seen as a futuristic technology, more associated with games and tech demonstrations than with fine art. But over the past few years, AR has increasingly established itself on the art scene, with exhibitions, public interventions, and experimental projects that push the boundaries between physical and digital experience. A few pioneering exhibitions have been especially important in making AR art visible to a broad public.

Apple's [AR]T Walk (2019)

One of the most influential early initiatives was Apple's collaboration with the New Museum in New York in 2019, called *[AR]T Walk*. The project brought AR art out of the gallery and into the city streets. In six cities—New York, London, Paris, San Francisco, Hong Kong, and Tokyo—visitors could join guided art walks where digital artworks appeared on their smartphones, layered over the urban landscape.

Seven international artists, including Carsten Höller, Nathalie Djurberg, and Pipilotti Rist, were commissioned to create site-specific AR works. Rist's piece, *International Liquid Finger Prayer*, transformed the city into a playful stage, where a shimmering form hopped across the streets, singing and teasing participants as they tried to catch it. Like many AR artworks, it blended sound, animation, text, and interactivity, creating an experience somewhere between art and game.

At the same time, Apple transformed more than twenty of its stores into temporary AR galleries. In each store, visitors could experience musician and artist Nick Cave's work *Amass*. The piece resembled a game where participants collected floating metallic objects in different shapes. Once all objects were gathered, the player unlocked a reward. *Amass* highlighted how AR could create playful, participatory experiences within a commercial space, while also introducing a new audience to digital art.

The First AR Biennale (2021)

If Apple's project represented AR's entrance into mainstream culture, the world's first AR art biennale, launched in Düsseldorf in the fall of 2021, marked its recognition in the institutional art world. Nineteen international artists were invited to create site-specific works for a new "sculpture park" that could only be accessed through visitors' smartphones.

One of the works, Jeremy Bailey's *YOUar*, appeared as a gigantic chrome bean lying on the grass. Visitors could "lift" the virtual sculpture, take selfies with it, and interact as if it were a physical object. The humor and accessibility of the piece demonstrated how AR can merge the aesthetics of public sculpture with the participatory culture of digital media.

Another contribution, *Digital Atmosphere* by the London-based studio Above&Below, showcased AR's potential to integrate real-time environmental data. Using digital sensors, the work measured air quality in Düsseldorf, translating invisible particles into a dynamic blue cloud of floating shapes. Visitors could watch the atmosphere around them visualized in real time, connecting AR to broader ecological concerns.

AR in Public Space: From Vävda Rum to Global Street Art

Augmented Reality (AR) has increasingly become a medium for public art, transforming cities and cultural spaces into interactive galleries. While early AR projects often took place in museums or tech showcases, recent initiatives have emphasized accessibility, interactivity, and engagement with urban environments.

One of the most notable Swedish projects is Vävda Rum, organized by Riksförbundet Sveriges Konstföreningar. Launched in 2023, it was Sweden's largest exhibition of virtual public art and the country's first national AR exhibition. Through a dedicated app, visitors could experience ten new interactive artworks in public spaces across nearly half of Sweden's municipalities, running from May 20 to September 30, 2023.

The artworks in *Vävda Rum* range from sculptural social networks and interactive reindeer herds to water sculptures whose appearance changes based on local weather data. Artists include Space Popular, Lundahl & Seitl, Oscar Häggström, Åsa Cederqvist, Untold Garden, Pastelae, Eric Magassa, James Webb, Adam James, and SONG. The project demonstrates how AR can turn public spaces into dynamic, immersive environments, making art accessible beyond traditional museum walls.

Other examples of public AR art include Vancouver's Mural Festival (2021), which integrated 24 murals with AR layers. Visitors could use their smartphones to see animations and interactive elements overlaying the painted walls. The festival highlighted how AR can revitalize street art, add narrative layers, and encourage exploration while adapting to pandemic-related restrictions on public gatherings.

Together, projects like *Vävda Rum*, the Vancouver Mural Festival, and the Düsseldorf AR Biennale illustrate a growing trend: AR is no longer a niche experiment but a platform for large-scale, participatory art. By combining digital technology with public spaces, these initiatives redefine how audiences encounter and interact with contemporary art, creating immersive experiences that are site-specific, playful, and socially engaging.

Chapter 10: Augmented Reality as a Tool for Activism

What if your artwork could hang next to the Mona Lisa at the Louvre, or right beside a masterpiece at MoMA in New York? While such access is normally reserved for a select few artists, Augmented Reality (AR) allows anyone to intervene in the museum space—virtually. Because AR art exists digitally and is only visible through a smartphone or tablet, it can be "placed" anywhere using GPS coordinates, opening new possibilities for artistic activism and intervention.

One striking example is the MoMAR project from 2021, where a group of artists used AR to position their works within the galleries of MoMA. These interventions, sometimes called "invasive sculptures," allowed artists to engage directly with the museum context without ever stepping inside. Among the participants was Tamiko Thiel, whose piece *ARt Critics Face Matrix* was part of this virtual guerilla action. By superimposing new layers onto existing museum spaces, the project questioned who gets to decide what is displayed and who the audience truly is.

AR as Commentary and Critique

AR has also been used to create critical commentary on high-profile exhibitions. In 2012, during Damien Hirst's retrospective at Tate Modern, Tamiko Thiel released an AR app that placed a virtual Hirst in a Christ-like pose while a rain of gold coins fell around him. This digital installation became a pointed, playful critique of Hirst's extravagant, market-driven art practice, exemplified by works like *For the Love of God*, the platinum skull encrusted with diamonds.

Similarly, AR allows artists to add layers of interpretation, satire, or protest to public artworks. When Jeff Koons partnered with Snapchat to release AR versions of his iconic steel sculptures—like the balloon dog in Central Park—the AR works were quickly "vandalized" by graffiti artist Sebastian Errazuriz, who sprayed virtual graffiti over the sculptures using the same GPS coordinates. Errazuriz's action raised a fundamental question: who truly owns the virtual public space? Is it controlled by large tech companies, or does it also belong to everyday users?

AR Graffiti and the Democratization of Public Space

AR offers a unique solution to a long-standing debate about graffiti and public art. Unlike traditional graffiti, which alters or damages physical property, AR allows artists to leave a visible, interactive mark in public space without permanent consequences. Apps now exist for creating AR graffiti, tagging virtual artwork to specific locations, and enabling others to experience it through their devices. Apps that allow users to "paint" the city digitally, creating layers of commentary, play, or activism that coexist with the physical world.

In this way, AR becomes a tool for democratizing access to cultural spaces, challenging established hierarchies, and expanding the possibilities for public intervention. It allows artists and activists to overlay new narratives onto familiar spaces, engage audiences in interactive critique, and rethink what it means to occupy both virtual and physical environments.

Chapter 11: Augmented Realities – KAWS, Nina Chanel Abney, and Lauren Moffatt

In the evolving landscape of contemporary art, augmented reality (AR) has emerged as a transformative medium, enabling artists to transcend traditional boundaries and engage audiences in immersive experiences. This chapter delves into the works of three prominent artists—KAWS, Nina Chanel Abney, and Lauren Moffatt —whose innovative use of AR has redefined artistic expression and audience interaction.

KAWS: Blurring the Lines Between Physical and Digital Realms

Brian Donnelly, known professionally as KAWS, has been at the forefront of integrating AR into his artistic practice. In collaboration with Acute Art, KAWS launched the "Expanded Holiday" project in 2020, introducing virtual versions of his iconic "Companion" sculptures in 12 cities worldwide, including New York, Paris, and São Paulo. These monumental AR installations allowed viewers to experience his signature characters in real-world settings through their smartphones.

Further expanding his digital presence, KAWS presented "NEW FICTION," his first major solo exhibition in London, in 2022. This exhibition featured both physical and AR works, including a collaboration with the popular video game Fortnite, where his sculptures were digitally integrated into the game's environment.

KAWS's innovative approach exemplifies how AR can bridge the gap between traditional art forms and digital platforms, engaging a broader audience and redefining the art-viewing experience.

Nina Chanel Abney: Social Commentary Through Augmented Narratives

Nina Chanel Abney, an American artist renowned for her vibrant and bold artworks, has adeptly incorporated AR to enhance her social commentary. In 2020, she collaborated with Acute Art to present "Imaginary Friend," an AR installation that placed her stylized characters in various global locations, including Paris and New York. These digital figures, characterized by their dynamic poses and expressive features, serve as vehicles for Abney's exploration of race, identity, and cultural narratives.

Abney's AR works invite viewers to engage with her art in public spaces, prompting reflection on societal issues through interactive experiences. By merging traditional painting techniques with cutting-edge technology, she creates a dialogue between the physical and digital realms, challenging audiences to reconsider their perceptions of art and its role in activism.

Lauren Moffatt — *Reverse Dive* (2023)

One of Lauren Moffatt's most significant augmented reality projects is *Reverse Dive: Local Knowledge, Partial Truth* (2023), created for the Non-Fungible Conference in Lisbon. The work transforms a public park into a site of speculative ecology and digital intervention. When viewed through a smartphone or tablet, visitors encounter a towering flower figure rising out of the landscape. Its petals slowly unfold, while surrounding architectural structures dissolve into vegetation, as if nature were reclaiming the built environment.

The piece reimagines AR not just as a tool for overlaying digital images onto the world, but as a means of rebalancing relationships between humans, plants, and public space. By positioning the flower as both monumental and delicate, Moffatt points to alternative value systems—where beauty, care, and interdependence become more important than speed, growth, and technological dominance.

Unlike many commercial AR projects that emphasize spectacle or entertainment, *Reverse Dive* situates augmented reality within a poetic and ecological framework. It invites viewers to slow down, reflect, and experience a form of shared space that is both virtual and rooted in the material world. Through this, Moffatt demonstrates how AR can act as a subtle form of activism—shaping not only what we see, but how we imagine our place within larger living systems.

Chapter 12: Museums, Art History, and Augmented Reality

Museums have always been places of storytelling—spaces where artworks are not only displayed but also interpreted and contextualized. With augmented reality (AR), museums now have powerful new tools to expand these narratives, creating interactive and immersive dialogues with visitors. Instead of passively looking at an artwork, audiences can experience it in layered ways, seeing hidden details, historical reconstructions, or even stepping virtually into the world of a painting.

One example is Rembrandt Reality, developed by the Mauritshuis museum in The Hague. This AR app transforms Rembrandt's *The Anatomy Lesson of Dr. Nicolaes Tulp* (1632) into a three-dimensional scene. By walking through their own living room with a smartphone, users find themselves transported into a 17th-century anatomy theater, circling around the dissected body while observing the figures from multiple perspectives. In this way, the painting becomes a living tableau, bridging past and present.

Another significant project is Google Arts & Culture's "Meet Vermeer", which brought together 36 of Vermeer's paintings from 18 museums worldwide. Using AR, visitors could project the entire exhibition into their own homes, walking through a digitally reconstructed gallery as if all of Vermeer's masterpieces were under one roof. This not only expanded access to art history but also showed how AR can create exhibitions unconstrained by geography.

Museums have also experimented with AR overlays on physical exhibitions. Some shows use "empty" frames that come alive with digital paintings when viewed through a device, while others animate existing works. Imagine a static still life that suddenly reveals the artist's sketches, or a portrait where the sitter speaks directly to the visitor. Instead of an audio guide, AR can provide interactive layers: highlighting brushstrokes, comparing versions of the work, or re-creating missing or damaged details.

Other institutions are exploring more experimental uses. The National Gallery in London has tested AR to show conservation processes, letting visitors peel back the layers of a painting to see its underdrawings. Archaeological museums use AR reconstructions to rebuild ruins, temples, and objects in their original form. Contemporary art museums are also commissioning AR works that interact with their collections, blurring the lines between history and innovation.

These examples suggest that AR is not only a tool for engagement but also a way of rethinking museum education. Instead of didactic wall texts, visitors can choose how deeply to explore an artwork—through animation, reconstruction, or storytelling. AR gives museums the possibility to make art history more accessible to younger audiences while also offering specialists new layers of research and interpretation.

In the future, museums may become hybrid spaces, where physical and digital realities overlap. An empty gallery could hold hundreds of different AR exhibitions over time, and a visitor standing in front of a painting could unlock countless narratives—art historical, personal, and speculative. Ultimately, AR is reshaping museums from static archives into dynamic platforms of dialogue, discovery, and imagination.

Chapter 13: Beyond VR and AR – Defining Immersive Art Through Experience

In the beginning of this book, we recalled the ancient contest between the painters Zeuxis and Parrhasius, who competed to see who could create the most convincing illusion. Zeuxis painted grapes so real that birds tried to peck at them, while Parrhasius painted a curtain so lifelike that Zeuxis himself was fooled. Their duel reminds us that art has always sought to blur the boundary between appearance and reality, challenging perception and asking: *What is real, and what is illusion?*

Today, this contest continues—only the tools have changed. Instead of pigments on canvas, artists work with virtual reality, augmented reality, and hybrid technologies. Yet the goal remains the same: to immerse the audience in an experience so convincing, so transformative, that they forget where the artwork ends and the world begins.

Experience Over Medium

In immersive art, the goal is not to showcase technology for its own sake, but to use it as a tool to create deep engagement. A viewer might inhabit an artwork physically, virtually, or both at once. The continuum between real and virtual dissolves, and what remains is a heightened state of interaction and presence. In this sense, immersive art is about transforming consciousness and perception, not just layering digital content onto the world.

Toward the Future of Immersive Art

The next wave of immersive art may not be tied to specific devices at all. With the rise of mixed reality glasses, AI-generated worlds, and haptic technologies, artists are gaining new tools to shape how we experience reality. Imagine artworks that adapt in real time to a viewer's heartbeat, brainwaves, or emotional state, or environments that combine live performance with dynamic virtual layers visible only through AR.

Crucially, immersive art will be defined less by whether it is "VR" or "AR," and more by how it engages imagination, perception, and participation. As technology becomes more seamless and integrated into daily life, the most radical immersive art may not feel like "technology" at all—but like stepping into an expanded version of reality itself.

www.ingramcontent.com/pod-product-compliance
Lightning Source LLC
Chambersburg PA
CBHW050024230526
45470CB00003B/1115